I *Don't* Want My Baby Back

The true story of how that song became that song.

By Guy Bommarito

First Edition

ISBN: 9798320278636

Cover illustration and design by Larry Martin.

To Hillary Clinton, Ken Dennis, and GSD&M, who one way or the other made this stupid song possible.

Preface

The Chili's Baby Back Ribs song should never have happened. But, it did.

After its first airing on network TV, that should have been the end of it. But, it wasn't.

After a second airing some months later, that *really* should have been the end of it. But, it still wasn't.

So, what happened?

What happened was funnyman Mike Myers used it as a one-off joke in the movie *Austin Powers: The Spy Who Shagged Me*. And, what happened after that was the one-off became a two-, three-, and four-off in other movies, TV shows, and entertainment venues that continues to this day.

"The Chili's Baby Back Ribs Song" is the jingle that refused to die.

The only thing more absurd is the story behind it.

Which brings me to the internet. The origin story of the song is all over the place on the web. If there is any single reason why I wrote this book, it was to set the record straight.

For starters, that meant getting the year it was written right: 1995. (An earlier Chili's Baby Back Ribs jingle that sounded nothing like the one everybody knows was produced in the mid-eighties. More on that in Chapter 6.)

Other than that, this book also attempts to clear up any other lesser ambiguities.

Except for the fact that the way the song came to be is so random, no one would have believed it if it hadn't actually happened.

I *Don't* Want My Baby Back

Introduction

When I was in high school, I had this friend —
let's call him "Jim" (because that was his real
name.) I hung out with Jim not so much because
we were buddies, but because we were buddies
with this other guy.

Jim was clearly the high achiever among us. A
straight "A" student and national merit scholar,
he later went to Harvard. (By contrast, our
mutual buddy went to Abilene Christian College
where he played football and, as an offensive
lineman, was once knocked on his ass so hard
that he had to ask the coach if he could go back
to the locker room and change his pants.)

Jim, on the other hand, graduated with Ivy
League honors the same week the University of
Texas handed me my "So-long-and-thanks-for-
the-tuition" lambskin with a degree in
Advertising.

Fast forward fifteen years. Jim is teaching
English at the University of Texas, and invites

me to speak to his class about how I do what I do. Since graduating, I've been a copywriter and creative director at various advertising agencies in Texas and California. I'd spoken with numerous ad classes at UT prior to this pending reunion, but never to an English class. "How different could it be?" I thought.

It was very different.

Ad classes treated me like a god when I showed them work that made them laugh or caught them off-guard with an unexpected ending. When I showed the same work to Jim's English class, all they wanted to know was how I justified manipulating the masses with what was clearly the devil's craft.

Jim was the worst of them. He asked me to come clean on the tricks that ad people employed to coerce consumers into doing things they would never have done under normal circumstances. For example, he asked, "Has everyone noticed how the logo is always in the bottom right corner of a print ad so that when you turn the page you have to look at it?"

What?

First, every print ad does not come with a pre-determined placement for the logo. And, even it if did, how would simply seeing it be a catalyst for any sort of action? (When you walk into a baseball stadium and see a Toyota logo next to the scoreboard, do you feel compelled to leave during the seventh-inning stretch to buy a Camry?)

It's like they were all channeling Vance Packard. So, I decided to tell them the truth, the whole truth, and nothing but the truth.

Ad agencies and their clients have enough trouble just getting everybody on the same page without adding "manipulate the masses with subliminal subterfuge" to their to-do lists. Writers fight with art directors, account people fight with creative directors, directors fight with producers, CMOs fight with everyone. It's a wonder we ever make a deadline.

Jim didn't believe me. His class didn't believe me. I couldn't get out of there fast enough.

Fast forward another ten years. After 25 years in the business, I'd had it — with clients who never met a focus group they wouldn't take it up the ass for, with account people who had "Whatever you say, sir or madam" tattooed on their foreheads, with creative departments less driven to think outside the box than to juggle the turds inside it, with production company directors who insisted on rethinking concepts over enhancing them, with agency principals who used their positions to bring back approved work that was never approved by anyone in the creative department...and on...and on.

In short, I was done with all of the things that Jim's class never took into consideration before blindly assuming that ad people spent their days looking for ways to airbrush (pre-Photoshop) the letters S, E, and X into the ice cubes in a glass of Wild Turkey.

I only mention this to set the stage for the story that lies ahead: no better example of the dysfunctional dynamic between ad agencies and their clients exists than the story behind the Chili's Baby Back Ribs song.

Like a lot of advertising, it has its roots in events no one ever would have predicted.

Least of all, me.

Chapter 1

"Houston, we have a problem"

I grew up in Houston, Texas. Along with trophy-size roaches and humidity that guarantees every day will be a bad hair day, until the latter part of the 20th century, being a Houstonian also meant living in a city with no professional sports teams at the major league level. In the 60s, the Houston Oilers made their debut in the nascent American Football League, and the Colt 45s (later, the "Astros") became one of two new expansion teams in Major League Baseball's National League. (The other team was the New York Mets, because having just one team clearly wasn't enough for the Big Apple — who'd only recently had three.)

The Oilers did well in their early years, winning the first two AFL championships. But, the upstart league hadn't yet achieved full legitimacy or acquired an entrenched fanbase, so those championships didn't lead to tickertape parades down Main Street or bragging rights outside the city limits.

Later, the city eventually gained an NBA team — the Houston Rockets — that would bring a national championship to the city, but not for another 30-plus years.

Unfortunately, for decades after the arrival of professional sports, being a sports fan in Houston was typically gut-wrenching. While the Astros rarely threatened to make the playoffs, the Oilers and Rockets occasionally did so, only to lose, often spectacularly, with the championship trophy within their reach.

Then, 1994 strolled in, and the Houston Rockets qualified for the playoffs as a sixth seed — not an auspicious way to begin a championship run, but at least they made it to the post season. And, to commemorate this milestone, the Rockets decided they needed a commercial.

As coincidence would have it, one of the executives with an ownership interest in the Rockets also happened to be very good friends with the "S" in GSD&M, the Austin, Texas, ad agency where I was executive creative director. That "S" was Roy Spence.

Roy was our bigger than life agency president whose presentations often came across as fiery sermons. Thus, his nickname: Reverend Roy.

Roy brought the Rockets' assignment to the agency in the spring of 1994, and I immediately saw it as an opportunity to do something special. The point of the spot was to thank Houston fans for their support. Easy enough. I put a creative group on it with the direction to go for the fences (to confuse metaphors.)

A few days later, the teams came into my office to show me their work. It not only missed the metaphorical fences, it never got out of the metaphorical infield. I sent them back to their drawing boards (not metaphorically back then.) Later that week they returned with a spot that I thought had the potential to really breakthrough.

The idea was to search for footage of Rockets' games where something totally unpredictable, unintended, or unanticipated occurred that somehow resolved itself in a spectacular way. (For example, a pass that bounced off the head of a costumed mascot on the sidelines only to inexplicably career off the backboard and end up in the basket.) Once we found something along those lines, we'd shoot what appeared to be actual game footage of the Rockets' coach drawing up what happened as an actual play *about* to happen and giving it to his players to execute.

The more bizarre the play, the funnier the spot would be. So, it was just a matter of searching through previously shot video to find those moments. But, before we could take the idea into production, we had to sell the concept to the client. It turned out that was easier said than done.

The client didn't care for the concept and, as a result, basically directed us to go back and bring him something more pedestrian. His big idea — which he gleefully shared with the agency — was putting individual players on camera thanking Houston for their support.

I don't think so.

"Look," I told the team, "We're not doing this just so Roy can get another signed jersey. If we can't do a spot that we love for a one-off project that we're probably going to lose money on anyway, we're not going to do anything."

Two days later, the team came back into my office to share their latest and greatest. There was some nice stuff, but nothing to write home about. "Anything else," I queried. Then, one of the writers said, "Well, I did have this idea where someone is listening to a Rockets game on a portable radio while standing on the ledge of a building like he was about to jump if they lost. But I couldn't figure out how to make it funny."

A punchline ending couldn't have resolved itself more instantly for me — the direct result of having watched way too many Road Runner cartoons as a kid. I couldn't get the words out of my mouth fast enough with regards to where we could take the spot from there.

"Okay," I said, "The guy is on the ledge listening to the game, and he has a rope tied around his ankle on one end that's attached to an anvil on the other. The Rockets are down a point with just enough time to win if they can make the final basket. A Rockets player shoots and misses, and the announcer says, 'He misses! Rockets lose!' The guy then says, 'That's it, I just can't take it anymore,' and he throws the anvil off the ledge — but it's attached to a long rope, and before it can completely unravel and take him down, the announcer says, 'But wait, he was fouled!' [indicating that the Rockets still had one more shot at a victory.] Quick cut to the guy's face, realizing that it's too late to undo what he's set in motion. Then, go to logo and say something like 'The Houston Rockets would like to thank their fans for their support this season, because we all know how tough it is being a sports fan in Houston.'"

We had our spot. I told the account people that this was it. The Rockets buy it or we tell them to do it themselves. (Something I could/would never do with any "real" clients whose billings actually kept us in business.)

The account team sold it. The creative team produced it. The spot turned out better than any of us imagined. And, the city of Houston fell in love with it. In fact, it was such a hit that during halftime at one of the Rocket's nationally-televised playoff games, one of the play-by-play announcers said, "There's a TV spot they've been running here in Houston in support of the Rockets that's captured the imagination of the city, and we're going to play it for you now."

And, that was the first and only time any TV spot I ever had anything to do with got free air time on a national broadcast.

What does any of this have to do with the Baby Back Ribs song? I'm getting there.

Chapter 2

"Houston, Hillary, and Healthcare"

It's a month later. The Rockets have won their first national championship. The spot did everything we hoped it would do and more. And, Roy is in Houston where he's gone to see an old college friend he met when they were part of a group of university students across the country working on the McGovern '72 presidential campaign.

Her name is Hillary Clinton.

Roy and the Clintons had been friends for over two decades. As college students, they slept on each other's couches in their respective apartments. When Bill Clinton was running for governor of Arkansas, Judy Trabulsi (one of Roy's then future partners at GSD&M who was part of that college crew) used to tell me without batting an eye that someday this person I'd never heard of was going to be president of the United States.

"I want to show you something we did for the Houston Rockets on their way to winning the NBA championship," Roy says to Hillary. He shows her the spot, and she reacts accordingly, laughing and applauding at its conclusion. "That's just the kind of commercial we need for our universal health care legislation," she responds. "Would you guys be interested in helping us out there?"

Would we like to work with the President and First Lady of the United States of America on a series of TV spots to help sell the American people on the idea of national health insurance? Yes. Yes, we would like that very much.

So, Roy comes back to Austin, tells us we'll be working with the First Lady on her healthcare initiative, and a few days later, we are sitting around the phone in his office on a conference call with Hillary Clinton. (It was as surreal to us then as I'm sure it sounds to you now.)

Once again, thanks to Roy's relationship with the Clintons and that Rockets spot, we found ourselves with another huge opportunity, and once again, I was determined to make the most of it.

We got to work.

After a few weeks we had a number of scripts we felt pretty good about. So, the next step was for Roy to lock down a presentation time that we were all assuming would take place via another conference call. Until Mrs. Clinton asks us if we'd like to come up to the White House to present in person.

Duh, yeah.

Chapter 3

"We're in the fucking White House"

No sooner does our limo pull up to the front gate when a bevy of security personnel surround the vehicle, sliding metal rods with upwards facing mirrors below the chassis to check for explosives. Once that little reindeer game is over, they do a walkaround with a couple of German shepherds sniffing for anything else with the potential to level a city block that the low-tech mirrors might have missed. In the interim, our IDs are checked, and at least half of us are biting our lips to keep from making a joke about whether the next thing on their to-do list is an anal probe. Satisfied that we aren't terrorists or Republicans, they give us the green light to proceed up the driveway to the iconic entrance familiar to anyone who's ever glanced at the back of a twenty-dollar bill.

We are about to enter the William Jefferson Clinton White House.

No sooner do we walk past the front doors than someone who knows more than we do about where we're supposed to be ushers us past the stare of presidential portraits hanging mute on the foyer walls to a small elevator situated off the main entry. (You would think a place like the White House would have some zippier form of transport between floors that doesn't leave you wondering if somewhere in the basement chipmunks are jogging on a treadmill. Then again, it is an old house.)

The elevator lifts us to an upper floor where our intrepid guide takes us down a hallway so narrow you could stick both arms out and almost touch the opposing walls at the same time. Which, of course, I attempt to do. Our final stop is a room called the Solarium.

We're told that the Solarium is the only room in the White House that the first family is allowed to decorate themselves. Perhaps that explains the blue gingham wallpaper. They are, after all, from Arkansas.

Once inside, Doug and Brian, the art director/writer team responsible for the first round of TV scripts that we have come to the White House to present, begin frantically looking for a place to plug in the portable printer we brought with us from Austin — just in case we made any last-minute changes on the plane ride up here, which we did. We hadn't planned on completely re-concepting and rewriting the work we spent weeks finalizing prior to the trip. But, Roy hadn't been personally involved in the creative process and, seeing the ideas for the first time on the flight up here, he felt the need to put his mark on them.

To be fair, the ideas are better now than they were when we boarded the plane.

As the scripts are printing, I notice a small stack of napkins imprinted with an illustration of the White House sitting on the table next to me. My first thought is "Who would wipe their mouth on a drawing of the White House?" My second thought is to surreptitiously stuff one into my pocket to pull out later as proof that I was really there.

As if on cue, that's when Mrs. Clinton walks in.

Dressed in a powder blue suit that could easily have come off the rack at JCPenney, she is all smiles, enthusiastically welcoming us and doing everything within her power to make us feel like sitting down with the First Lady of the United States is something we all do on a regular basis.

The Republicans have already beaten the Clinton administration to the airwaves with a series of devastatingly effective TV spots — popularly being referred to as the "Harry & Louise" campaign — featuring a middle-aged couple fretting over how health coverage for all Americans would be akin to the Bataan Death March for seniors.

Before we can get started, however, an older African-American gentleman in a white suit straight out of wardrobe from the set of *Gone with the Wind* comes in with a plate covered in aluminum foil. He places it on the far end of a dining table on the other side of the room and leaves without explanation. No one else seems to notice but me.

We've been told for weeks now that Mrs. Clinton will be the only Clinton in the meeting. In the middle of pleasantries with the First Lady, however, the President of the United States unexpectedly walks in.

"Don't pay attention to me," Mr. Clinton says amidst the hugs, hellos, and silent "Holy Fuck, the president just walked in"s. "This is Hillary's meeting," he concedes. "I'm just here to watch." Right. So, we're just going to ignore the donkey in the room. (Using the elephant analogy for a Democratic president didn't seem quite right here.) He then parks himself behind the covered plate set out for him moments earlier and rolls the foil back where something resembling a piece of fish will be the leader of the free world's dinner tonight.

"I can't wait to see what you've done," the first lady exclaims. She sits back, and that's our cue to see if we can impress two of the most powerful people on the planet in the next half hour. No pressure.

Roy starts things off, keeping things light and informal before tossing the grenade, er ball, to me. While I've made hundreds of presentations in my career to everyone from founders to chairmen and other senior muckety-mucks of companies like Southwest Airlines, Coca-Cola, and Wal-Mart, this is definitely different.

Mrs. Clinton turns out to be a terrific audience. She gets what we're trying to do, laughs at the right times, and says what you'd want a client to say after seeing the work. Mr. Clinton does much the same, diplomatically waiting for his better half to comment before chiming in, lest he be accused of commandeering the meeting with a separate agenda.

The presentation goes very well. They like the work. A bit surprisingly, Mrs. Clinton seems to have a better grasp of what we're trying to do with some of the finer points than the president does, and takes the liberty of explaining the subtle nuances of one of the concepts he doesn't quite get. The discussion is interrupted when someone wheels a large TV set (remember those?) into the room, and the president says, "Hillary was interviewed by Tom Brokaw earlier today. Do you mind if we watch it?"

I think that's what you call a rhetorical question.

It's a bit bizarre watching the First Lady and President of the United States watching her responding to questions on TV about their efforts to pass a revolutionary health care bill. But, not quite as bizarre as when the camera cuts to a close-up of Mrs. Clinton compelling the president to shatter the silence in the room with "Isn't she pretty?" Nobody so much as clears their throat, and somehow, the room feels even more silent after that.

They ask us to take the scripts into production. Mission accomplished. (Or, so we thought. More on that to come.)

On the way out, the president says, "Wait, a second, I have to pee." (Yes, he really did say that.) We wait in the hall while we listen for his stream to stop. Once we hear his zipper return to its full and upright position, he strides out and meets back up with us for the ride down the elevator to the first floor.

Back in the foyer again, I find myself standing next to the portrait of John F. Kennedy to my left and six inches from the 42nd president's ear on my right. He is telling us a story about the time a reporter in Alabama tried to stump him with a question on abortion and the Bible. In that instance, I immediately understand how William Jefferson Clinton got elected to the highest office in the land. Bill Clinton has something you and I don't. It's not evident on TV, but in his presence, it's unmistakable.

After a few minutes of presidential banter, Mrs. Clinton interrupts her better half with "Now, now, we have to let these people go. They have a plane to catch." (And, some of *us* could use a bathroom break too.)

We exit the White House through the same gate that let us in, albeit this time, without the cameras and canines. We're all dumbstruck at what just happened when Roy — sensing the need to say something commensurate with the moment — says, "Well, that was a mind fuck." We all nod at the understatement, and then Roy asks the driver to stop by the nearest liquor store so we can self-medicate on the flight back to Austin.

The seed for the Chili's Baby Back Ribs song had been planted.

Chapter 4

"The trip hits the fan"

Back in the office the next morning, the meeting with the President and Mrs. Clinton still seems like a dream when I get a phone call from my creative team working on a Chili's TV shoot in Los Angeles.

The client is not happy.

We'd had the Chili's account for six years up to that point, and unfortunately for me, Ken Dennis, the marketing director felt very strongly that I, as Executive Creative Director, needed to be present at every production. As a result, I usually was. But, I wasn't going to miss a trip to the White House, and so on this one occasion, I sent along a highly competent senior team in my place. It wasn't enough.

"Where's Guy?" the marketing director asked.

"You're not going to believe this," my senior art director replied without thinking about the ramifications of what was about to come out of his mouth. "He went to the White House last night to present scripts to the Clintons to help them with the national health insurance bill they're trying to get through Congress."

They might as well have told him that I had flown to Dallas to have a sexual rendezvous with his wife. When it came to eruptions, Vesuvius could take lessons from Ken.

A little back story.

Brinker International, the company that owned the Chili's Grill & Bar concept, was a very conservative organization. Atilla the Hun would have been right at home as a board member. Founder Norm Brinker's two best friends were George H.W. Bush and Ross Perot. During H.W.'s tenure, Norm used to fly to the White House on Fridays to have lunch with the president.

In addition to being famous for creating the salad bar and "Hi, my name is Phil, I'll be your waiter today," Norm was very old school, and the school was clearly situated on a Southern campus. His company looked like a boys' club packed with young execs from "Yuppies 'r Us." All white, no long hair (trimmed mustaches were tolerated), and one token woman in anything other than support positions.

"Do you have any idea how much universal health insurance is going to cost us if we have to cover every Chili's employee?" Ken bellowed. Not really interested in waiting for an answer, he quickly followed that up with an ultimatum, "If Norm finds out about this, you guys are gone." He then capped off his if-the-last-thing-I-said-didn't-get-your-attention-this-next-thing-will statement with: "If you want to keep this account, you'll walk away from this right now."

If we wanted to keep the account?

Well, let's see. GSD&M's biggest accounts at the time were Southwest Airlines, Wal-Mart, Coors Beer, and some regional Coca-Cola business. But none of those accounts came anywhere close to delivering the profit margin we made on Chili's. If we lost Chili's, massive repercussions (layoffs, gnashing of teeth, never ending winters) would follow.

So, all we had to do now was call the First Lady and President of the United States and say, "Just kidding about all that work we showed you last night, but good luck with that health insurance thingy."

Fortunately, Roy had another rabbit he could pull out of his derriere.

After assuring Chili's that we'd walk away from the Clinton project, we got on the phone with Hollywood producers Harry and Linda Bloodworth Thomason. In addition to enjoying huge success with their *Designing Women* TV series, the Thomason's were active in Democratic Party efforts and generous with their time, particularly on projects that had anything to do with video production. We told them our predicament, handed them the scripts, and six weeks later Peter Jennings was talking about the finished spots on ABC's evening newscast.

Bullet dodged.

But, we were no longer bulletproof in Ken's eyes. And, we knew that we had to deliver and then some to get out of the Chili's doghouse.

Which we did. Until we didn't.

Chapter 5

"So, it's like this. You're fired."

Chili's produced several rounds of TV spots a year. Productions usually included spots for fajitas, burgers, a new menu item, and baby back ribs. The procedure was always the same. Ken would give us the go ahead to begin concepting. We'd develop scripts. Then, he and his "yes minions" would approve two directions for a formal presentation to the executive committee, who would then choose the winning campaign.

Who said advertising isn't glamorous?

Like most clients, Chili's gave the usual lip service to demanding "great" work — right up until the moment we presented scripts that didn't fit precisely to a formula that included some combination of "bite and smile" — people on the verge of orgasm because they are so thrilled with putting something from Chili's kitchen in their mouths, intercut with shots of that food being prepped, prepared, and presented to the guest(s) by the happiest waitpersons on the planet. Without those touchpoints, a chorus of "back in the box, back in the box" quickly followed, paving the way for spots that were always more mainstream than breakthrough.

As a result, nobody particularly loved or hated the spots we did after they aired because nothing about them really stood out.

Unfortunately, when agencies find themselves in a situation like this, here's what does *not* happen next: clients do *not* point the finger at themselves and say, "Our fault for making the agency do what they did." No, they point the finger at the agency and say, "That agency doesn't do very good work." And, they're right.

Agencies are responsible for the work they do even when clients cut the legs out from under anything resembling an idea. Part of what determines the worth of an agency is its ability to navigate around the obstacles constantly thrown in its path.

In other words, if an ad agency wants to do great work, it has to figure out how to do great work in an environment where the people who cut the checks really don't define "great work" the same way that it does. And, on that count, as hard as we tried, we were not doing work anywhere nearly as good as we wanted to do or should have been doing for Chili's.

So, after several years, that's where things stood between GSD&M and Chili's. The first round of creative was "out of the box." The second round based on the client's response to the first round was "back in the box." Then, it was our fault for under-delivering.

The year was 1995.

We were clearly at a point where we had to find a way to deliver something over and above our past work, regardless. Plus, still pissed off about that Clinton meeting, some of the management team was just looking for an excuse to jettison us. As a result, this time the direction wasn't just to "do great work," it was to "do what we think is great work or else."

After weeks of concepting and a handful of presentations, the winning campaign was a series of spots that came to be known as "Smell-O-Vision."

The idea behind Smell-O-Vision was that Chili's had come up with new technology that allowed people to smell the food they were watching on their TVs by scratching their TV screens — a not-so-subtle nod to the "Scratch 'N Sniff" print ads of the time. The scripts were, obviously, tongue-in-cheek, and actually pretty funny. The client was nervous, but feeling the pressure to deliver something apart from what they had done in the past, they approved the idea.

We produced it. It ran. And, for the first time in the history of our relationship with Chili's, sales actually went down. (It didn't help that some viewer's kid actually scratched their TV screen and damaged it so badly that Chili's agreed to buy them a new one.)

So, Chili's did exactly what they told us they were going to do. They fired us.

Chapter 6

"Why say it, when you can sing it?"

Back on a plane again — this time a Southwest Airlines 737 — we made our way up to Dallas to meet with Ken to beg for a second chance. Losing this account was simply not an option.

So, Roy, me, and Steve Gurasich — the "G" in "GSD&M" — walked ever so humbly into Ken's office to plead our case. Ken liked us, but not enough to come to our defense when our stock had taken such a nose-dive. The truth is, his job security was as perilous as ours if the club of whiteboys senior to him couldn't go to cocktail parties without friends and acquaintances constantly telling them how unimpressive their commercials were.

Fortunately, whatever equity we still had with Ken was enough, because after making our case, he decided to cut a short-term deal with us — but not without conditions. "Okay, here's the deal," he started out, "We need a :30 spot for baby back ribs and a :30 spot for our chicken entrees for a media buy starting in eight weeks. *And, we want both spots shot in the restaurant and driven by an original music track.* Give us those two spots, and we'll put off the decision to fire the agency for the time being."

In other words — correction, in exactly those words — Ken mandated that we produce two spots *driven by jingles* to keep the account.

Relieved at the reprieve we'd been granted, we agree. Duh. We'd have agreed to ride a longhorn wearing nothing but spurs on our butt cheeks down Dallas's Central Expressway to keep the account. We assure Ken that we will not disappoint him.

Steve is relieved. Roy is relieved. I am only semi-relieved. We got to keep the account, but only under the condition that we deliver my worst nightmare: a jingle-driven slice-of-life spot. The kind of ads I'd spent my entire career trying to avoid — and I wasn't alone.

In 1995, the lowest form of advertising was anything that had to do with a jingle. The heyday of the jingle was well past its "sell-by" date. Respectable agencies no longer did "You'll wonder where the yellow went when you brush your teeth with Pepsodent," "See the USA in your Chevrolet," or "I'm stuck on Band-Aid brand 'cause Band-Aid's stuck on me."

Some less than stellar agencies still did jingles, and they were all terrible. (Both the agencies and the jingles.) One highly-respected, creatively-driven agency in Los Angeles went so far as to do a holiday card to reinforce how low jingles had sunk on the creative totem pole. On the front of the card, prominent blanks preceded the word "bells" as in "_____ Bells, _____ Bells!" When you opened the card, the inside read "We don't do jingles."

It was in this environment that I was now given a "deliver a jingle-driven spot or else" assignment. I knew only one thing for certain. The last thing I could do if I was to retain any credibility with my creative department was to give the assignment to any one of them.

Which meant that I had to do it myself.

That left me with two options. I could contact a music production house and give the assignment to them. But, if I did that, I was basically assured of getting the same hackneyed work that the assignment called for. Or, I could try to write something myself that I didn't hate.

To make matters worse, Chili's had previously produced a blues-driven jingle for their original baby back ribs commercials through a music production house in Dallas a decade earlier that the client liked a lot. The jingle featured a Louie Armstrong clone singing "I love my baby back ribs." (In fact, it was a 70-something white guy who specialized in sounding black. More on that later.) So, whatever I did, it was going to be compared internally to that.

I had written a few pieces of music before. Prior to my first composition, however, the process of creating a piece of music was a complete mystery to me. Where did it come from? How did the words and music come together? And speaking of words and music, does one come before the other?

Then one day, everything fell into place for me. Words have a sound when you string them together: inflections, a rhythm, the words we emphasize to make a point. And, music is what those strings of words sound like. Once you listen for it, it couldn't be more obvious. To illustrate my point, here are the lyrics to the first song I ever wrote.

"I wanna barf on my shoes,
'Cause I drank too much booze.
My breath smells like a goat.
My dinner's stuck in my throat.
Tryin' to barf on my shoes.

"I wanna barf on my shoes.
'Cause I drank too much booze.
I don't understand
I've almost swallowed my hand
Trying to barf on my shoes."

Okay, it's not Lennon/McCartney. But once I had the words, I found corresponding musical notes that flowed as effortlessly as speaking. Once the code was broken, I knew I could write a better piece of music than 99% of the jingle writers out there, even if I'd never done it before. (Now that's what you call hubris.)

When we got back to the Austin, I went into my office, shut the door, picked up my pen and for reasons I don't understand to this day, both the words *and melody* to the baby back ribs jingle spilled out simultaneously.

"I want my baby back, baby back, baby back,
I want my baby back, baby back, baby back…
Chili's baby back ribs
Chili's baby back ribs
Barbecue sauce
Chili's Baby Back Ribs
Chili's Baby Back Ribs
Barbecue sauce
I want my baby back ribs."

I was done in less than five minutes.

Chapter 7

"There's no right way to write music"

Okay, before we go any further, let's deal with the 800-pound gorilla on lead guitar in the room. How does someone who barely understood the process behind songwriting write something in less than five minutes that eventually became iconic?

It's less absurd than it sounds, but to understand that, first you have to understand a little bit about the creative process.

Most people — including most creative people — don't have a clue how the creative process works. Until I was invited to teach a class on creativity at the University of Texas, neither did I. Little, by little, however, I came to find the words that explained the mystery along with what makes it so mysterious.

The creative process manifests itself in one of two ways: 1. Poof! And 2. Stumble.

An idea either comes to you from out of nowhere (Poof!), or it's the product of a series of irrational meanderings that lead you to stumble onto something you never would have thought of in a rational, logical manner. Thus, my definition of creativity: nonsense in search of a breakthrough.

Clearly, my musical revelation was a product of "Poof!"

The same thing happened to Bob Dylan (with far more impressive results) when he wrote "Like a Rolling Stone." To hear him retell it, he was walking by his kitchen table where a pad of paper and a pencil were already cocked and ready when he sat down and "the words just started pouring out like vomit."

My vomit just happened to have barbecue sauce on it.

The Baby Back Ribs song was an aberration on a number of levels. For example, when you write lyrics to a song, words and music don't necessarily come together at the same time.

For those composers where words come first, step two is finding a sound to go with them. Since writing a good song is basically the ability to match the words with the emotions inherent in their meaning, the more interesting the words, the more likely the composer will find a corresponding sound that elevates those words on an magical level.

Given the words to "Chili's Baby Back Ribs Song," it would have been virtually impossible to write them without the melody at the same time — because by themselves, the words are basically a series of repetitive phrases that don't contain enough emotional substance to suggest a tune. In fact, without music, the words consist of little more than "I want my baby back ribs." So, I was fortunate that both the words and music came to me simultaneously.

To further illustrate, here's a set of lyrics I wrote a few years earlier (under duress) for Coors beer before handing them over to a composer to finish out with a melody. Note how these words give a composer quite a bit more to work with. (Also note, that I hated this assignment and wouldn't have done it if my creative director hadn't put me in a position where I had to deliver.)

"Like cruisin' in the front seat of a hot pink Coup de Ville,
Like cut-off jeans and beauty queens
And a hundred-dollar bill.
I'm an American original
I drink Coors beer in a can
Drink an ice-cold Coors with a friend of yours
Put a cold draft beer in your hand."

Having gotten lucky with the way the words and music for the Baby Back Ribs song came together, next on the to-do list was some music and words for Chili's chicken offerings.

Nothin'.

I heard nothin'. No words. No music. I had no idea of where to go with a jingle about chicken menu items.

So, I started writing aimlessly in hopes of "stumbling" onto a direction that might take me somewhere. Minutes later I somehow ended up parroting the lyrics from Harry Nilsson's "(Put The Lime In The) Coconut" — as in "Put the chicken on the grill..." Unfortunately, that song then became so ingrained in my head, I couldn't tap into another melody no matter how hard I tried.

And, trying never works when you're "trying" to create something.

Maybe we could buy the Nilsson song, I thought. Maybe not. With no inkling of where to take the chicken song, I decided that exploring the possibility of buying the rights to the lime/coconut song from the Nilsson estate would be our best strategy for now.

Next step: sing it, sell it, produce it.

Chapter 8

"Barbecue Saaaaaaaauce!"

"I just wrote a jingle for baby back ribs," I confess to my wife, Mimi, over the phone. Mimi worked downstairs in GSD&M's PR department. "Oh, yeah," she replies, "Sing it to me." So, Mimi becomes the first person on the planet to hear "Chili's Baby Back Ribs Song."

"That's really cute," she says. She doesn't know it, but the word "cute," is the one word a creative person hates to hear when presenting an idea. It's not her fault. "Cute" just happens to be the default word everyone not in an advertising creative department uses when they like something they see or hear in the world of advertising. It's a compliment, and it's a whole lot better than "That sucks," so I don't press her further and allow my ego to declare victory.

Next up, Steve Gurasich. "Hey, got a second, Steve-O?" (If he can call me "Bombo," I can call him "Steve-O.") "Whatcha got, Bombo?" I sing for the big guy. "Is there instrumentation behind it?" I assure him that while it sounds like it was written acapella, and it works acapella, it may need some melodic or percussive embellishment that we'd work that out in the production.

Steve's cool with it. Next stop, Dallas.

We fly up later that week to do the dog and pony for Ken and Doug, another Brinker honcho who broke into the Chili's ranks managing Chili's first stores with Ken. I set up the song. I sing the song. Ken is concerned that it sounds too much like "four guys harmonizing on a Philadelphia street corner" and could feel too much like early rock and roll, which does not relate in any way to Chili's culture or the tone of any past work. I assure him that my intention is to contemporize it.

No one appears to be overly impressed, but they give it their thumbs up anyway.

Let me repeat that. NOBODY who first heard the song thought that I'd written anything approaching the iconic piece of advertising it was to become. Least of all me. The highest accolade it got from anyone up to that point was "Yeah, that should work."

As for the "chicken as a category" song, all I had at that point was a set of lyrics I wrote sans melody with the plan being to either convince the Nilsson estate to sell us the rights to their song or find a music house to fill in the missing notes. Since Ken and Doug had no issue with the lyrics, we were off to the races there too.

With approvals in hand, I now had to get the songs produced.

The head of broadcast production at GSD&M was a seasoned, often skeptical bordering on cynical woman named Dorothy. Dorothy had seen it all, done it all. So, when I tell her I wrote music and lyrics for one song and just the lyrics for another one, and that my intention is to give the former to a production house to execute my vision while reaching out to the Nilsson estate to see if we can purchase the rights to "Coconut" for the chicken jingle, she takes notes without comment.

"How's the ribs spot go?" she inquires. I oblige with yet another live performance. She shows neither admiration nor disdain for my assault on her ears. "Who do you want to use?" "Tom Faulkner," I reply. "You sure?" she asks, "Tom can be such a pain in the ass."

Tom is a highly-talented songwriter/musician in Dallas, who could be a bit difficult at times. Not because he was a prima donna or ego-driven, but because he was a worrier. He fretted over every aspect of a piece of music, and all of his second guessing could be a drag sometimes. He was also exceptionally talented. Given the opportunity, he always made anything we brought to him better. "I wanna use Tom," I tell her.

Another thing about Tom? He never let me down.

"Do you want to call Tom or do you want me to?" Dorothy asks. "I'll call him." "Okay, after you talk to him tell him to call me so we can work out the details," she replies.

I get on the phone with Tom and tell him what I need. Silently, I'm thinking to myself that once Tom records the music, I will never have to personally sing the song again. But, when I sing it for Tom for what I hope is my final performance, the first thing he says is "Wait a minute, I want to record you to get the melody down before I begin." I sing it once more for his reel-to-reel for what I'm sure will be the last time I'm ever asked to do so. Again.

"Got it," he says. "I can probably get to it later this week. Do you want to come up for it?"

"Do I need to?" I ask.

"Not unless you want," he replies.

"Great. Just send me the tape when you're done."

Chapter 9

"What's black & white and racist all over?"

Nilsson is dead, and his estate doesn't want anything to do with an advertising jingle. I can't blame them. Neither did I. But it leaves me with a second song to create, so I throw that one to Tom as well.

"Here are the lyrics," I said, "It's all yours."

A week later I get a call from Tom. "I finished recording the music for the Chili's spots last night," he reports. "Great, let's hear it," I respond. He plays the Baby Back Ribs song first.

Tom has done something quite ingenious with the song. Realizing the need for a percussion track to drive the melody, he starts out with a spoon clanging against a glass to establish the beat before his voice intros the first line.

"I want my baby back, baby back, baby back…"

When the last line is sung, Tom has also added some "do do-id dooo do-do"s filling out the ending before the final sing-out "I want my baby back ribs."

He did a great job.

As for the chicken song, Tom recorded that too, and unfortunately, it sounds pretty much like I thought it would — like just one more insipid jingle. It's fine. But there's definitely no magic happening in that one. I don't have a clue what else to do with it. So, rationalizing that both spots will be forgotten a month after they run anyway, I decide to just finish up everything as best I can and get this dreadful assignment behind me.

Cassettes (remember those?) are sent to Ken for his approval. After hearing both spots for the first time, he approves the Baby Back Ribs song without much comment beyond, "Yeah, that's fine." As for the chicken music, he isn't quite as happy with that and wonders if Tom should add some steel drums to the track. Tom is adamant that steel drums would make it sound too Caribbean and after some back and forth, Ken approves the chicken music as is too.

Music approved. All we need now is a director to shoot the spots.

After considering several production companies for the spots, we decide to stay in Texas for budgetary reasons and go with Jeff Bednarz. Jeff is out of Dallas too. He's funny, he's energetic, he has a great eye, he's terrific with talent, and we are very lucky to have nailed him down because he is usually booked up.

Casting begins shortly thereafter, and that's where things get interesting again. The spec sheet calls for mostly young men who look like they could work in a Chili's kitchen, plus a young woman who might pass for waitstaff. The Dallas talent pool is not as deep as LA or NY, but then we're not looking for the next Meryl Streep.

When we review the tape from the day's session, we're all thinking the same thing. First, it appears like we have some very good choices. And second, most of the better ones are African-American. That wasn't a problem for us. But, in the past, casting African-Americans was an issue with Norm Brinker.

The first baby back ribs jingle that Chili's aired in the mid-80s featured a white male who sounded uncannily like a black male in order to capture the bluesy sound the company wanted without coloring outside the corporate lines Norm dictated. I don't know if Norm was racist. I do know that Brinker International was a reflection of Norm, and any time we considered casting anyone but WASPs (who, not uncoincidentally, all looked very much like they lived in North Dallas), we were told that Norm wouldn't approve it.

We decided to push our selects anyway: three African-American and two Anglo males for the kitchen staff and one female of ambiguous ethnic background for the principal waitperson. Fingers crossed, we then sent the tape to Ken with a personal note telling him why we liked the talent we chose and asking him up front if Norm was going to have a problem with a primarily black cast.

The answer came back the next day. To our surprise, everyone was approved. The blacks were kitchen staff, not dining in the restaurant. So, we were told, no problem.

I'm sorry, but what year was this?

Writing about how this all went down as cavalierly as I just have is both painful and embarrassing. I'd like to say that dealing with issues of race the way we did was the only choice we had, but we could have said, "No." We could have chosen not to work with racists. But, we told ourselves that this was the playing field, and if we wanted to play, we had to deal with these issues the best way we knew how.

Basically, I/we had two choices. Quit. Or, use what influence we had to get the client to make the right decision. Because this kind of prejudice was so common in Texas, quitting every time someone revealed their racial biases would have left a lot of us unemployed for long stretches.

Let me set the stage a little better.

I grew up in Houston, Texas, in the 50s. Houston back then was a place where water fountains were labeled "white" and "colored," and blacks sat at the back of the bus. The only time I saw African-Americans in my neighborhood was when open air garbage trucks rolled down the street while a half a dozen or so "garbage men" in the bed of the truck stomped down on freshly emptied trash to make room for more. Neighborhood dogs announced their arrival like Armageddon had arrived.

My neighbor was a member of the John Birch Society. The "n word" was spoken as commonly and effortlessly as the word "y'all." I didn't learn that blacks had once been enslaved until I was introduced to it in my fourth-grade history book, and when I reported what I learned in school and how shocked I was about it in the family car on the way to church one Sunday, my father pulled over so he could yell at me for having the gall to express empathy for a group of people who were more closely aligned with the ape family tree than the human one.

The message growing up was clear. Blacks are not like whites. Yet, as much as I wanted to be a good son and buy into what I was being told, my gut begged to differ. I knew this line of thinking was bullshit. By the time I got to college and started reading everyone from James Baldwin to Malcom X and confronted my father with his bigotry, the chasm that always kept us from having the father/son relationship we both would have cherished became a canyon. At one point, I recall telling him that the world was changing, and he could change with it or stay behind as the rest of us went on without him.

That talk went well.

This Brinker situation was just another brick in that wall. It was always going to be us and them when it came to race relations in Texas. I just tried to do what was right and moved on.

Chapter 10

"Just when we thought it was done, it wasn't"

With the commercial cast, we shot both spots in a day on location in Chili's original restaurant on Greenville Avenue in Dallas. When you shoot a commercial that's supposed to look like people are singing live on the set, what's actually happening is an audio track is being played back during every take with the actors lip-syncing to it. As is usually the case, each scene in spots like these are shot multiple times to get just the right performance within various camera framings, and with each take there is audio playback. Which meant that we heard the song a lot that day — easily over a hundred times.

The spot had yet to run, and we were already sick of it.

Commercials shot. Edits made. Colors corrected. Titles added. The Chili's Baby Back Ribs spot debuted in the spring of 1995. It ran on national TV with a medium-heavy schedule for about six weeks. Then, it went away for a while. If it got any buzz, I never heard it.

Fortunately, sales went back up, and the talk of firing GSD&M went away as well. We were back to business as usual with Chili's.

The Baby Back Ribs spot ran again a number of months later and in a third network flight following that. Then, it went away (forever, I thought) to make way for the next Chili's campaign. Along with me. I left GSD&M in 1998 — burnt out and wrung out from daily confrontations with clients, creatives, and principals that never seemed to completely resolve themselves.

Up until that point, however, I never heard anyone outside of Tom Faulkner's voice sing the song. I never heard anyone even talk about it. Like most of our spots, it ran, it did whatever it was supposed to do, and if it was really good, we entered it in award shows.

We never entered the Baby Back Ribs spot in a single show. No one internally was that impressed either.

That all changed when *Saturday Night Live*'s Mike Myers decided he needed the song in the follow-up to his first very successful *Austin Powers* movie.

Enter, Fat Bastard.

Chapter 11

"Austin Powers comes to Austin"

Freelancing in Austin, still uncertain of what I wanted to do when I grew up, and well shy of being independently wealthy, I decided that milking the advertising cow would continue to be my default position until I could decide what to do next with my life.

Standing in line at the movies one afternoon, I run into the account supervisor I worked with on the Chili's account. After raising our eyebrows in simultaneous salutes upon recognizing a familiar face and syncing our "hellos," out of nowhere she says, "Hey, your song is going to be in a movie."

What?

"What song?" I asked. "What movie?" I asked again, as her end of the line continued its continental drift in the opposite direction of mine.

"The Baby Back Ribs song. It's going to be in the new *Austin Powers* movie." She's almost shouting now as our positions in line continue to extend in opposite directions.

What?

I needed to talk to Tom Faulkner and find out what was going on.

Back in the office, I phone Tom. "Oh, yeah," he says, "I've been meaning to call you. Okay, here's what happened."

What happened was that several months prior to my chance conversation with the account hostess, Tom got a call from an underling at GSD&M asking him if he had the contract for the Chili's Baby Back Ribs' music that had, at that point, been put to bed four years ago. "Yeah," he tells her, "But it's filed away somewhere. I'll have to look for it." "No problem," she says, "Just let us know when you get it."

Two days later, a second call came in from same young woman. "Did you find that contract yet?"

"No," Tom tells her. "I've been really busy and haven't had a chance to look for it yet."

She hangs up. The next day, another call.

"Okay," Tom says, "What's going on here. Why are you in such dire need to see a contract from a project done four years ago?"

She finally comes clean and tells him that the producers of the new *Austin Powers* movie had called Chili's and asked for permission to use the Baby Back Ribs song. Which meant Chili's contacted GSD&M to get clarification on what their rights were with regards to the music. Which explained why Tom was contacted.

As an outside supplier, unlike me at the time, Tom had some legal standing as to what was done with work he produced, whereas everything I created at the agency belonged to the agency and its clients — which accounts for those paychecks I used to get twice a month.

Tom explained to the young woman how all his contracts stipulated that while buyers own the music he produces for them, it's theirs — and here's the part that you can bet was underlined and in italics — ***for advertising purposes only.*** In other words, if Chili's or GSD&M wanted to give the *Austin Powers* people permission to use the song, they had to pay off Tom first.

Ka-Ching!

After some back and forth that I was not privy to, Tom asked for $4,000 plus a credit at the end of the movie citing him and me for our contribution, specifically: "Music by Tom Faulkner. Lyrics by Guy Bommarito."

That attribution, of course, was not quite accurate. Along with the words, I also wrote the bassline and melody before giving it to Tom, who did his usual phenomenal job of polishing everything up in production.

That said, when Tom told me what he had done, my biggest concern wasn't how he took credit for writing the song, it was what he was going to do with the $4,000. "I'll split it with you," he volunteered before I had to ask.

And, he did. And, the movie came out. And, as promised, both of our names were in the final credits. And, we couldn't believe how cool that was. And, that was it.

Or, so I thought.

Chapter 12

"There's that song again"

The song explodes.

After the *Austin Powers* premier, Mike Myers is on David Letterman showing previews of his latest masterpiece. Featured in the preview is an obese Scottish character played by Myers appropriately named Fat Bastard, who has decided that he wants to eat a miniature version of the main character (Dr. Evil) called "Mini Me." To reinforce the point, he starts singing "I want my baby back..." It gets a huge laugh from the studio audience.

The stage was set. In the months that followed, the "one-time" thing that I thought would go away in a few months started becoming a "there's that song again" thing.

As time went on, I once again had a front row seat to some of what was happening behind the scenes at GSD&M. After leaving the agency in 1998, I found myself back there in 1999, once again as lead creative on the Chili's account. (My sabbatical didn't accomplish quite what I'd hoped for, and the idea of replenishing my bank account while I continued my quest seemed like a prudent one.)

While the Chili's commercial featuring the song was no longer airing, requests continued trickling in for permission to use it in other venues. And, each time a request came in, the agency had to negotiate with Tom — who by now had assured himself of a cut of the pie by setting himself up as the sole composer of the song by registering it on BMI/ASCAP in his name exclusively. It didn't feel like that big a deal to me at the time so I didn't say or do anything about it. Besides, I was back on GSD&M's payroll, and I didn't see any benefit in making a fuss with Tom. I thought what Tom did was poor form, but I also still thought that it was just this stupid song that would go away at any moment.

The agency hated negotiating with Tom to use a piece of music they misguidedly felt was rightfully theirs to do with as they pleased. I recall going to bat for him with the account and broadcast teams at the agency more than once, telling them in so many words to "just get over it." Jingle composers rarely have something they produced go mainstream. This was Tom's big moment, I told them. Pay him.

Eventually, Tom and Chili's came to some agreement releasing his claim to future earnings. I have no idea what transpired there, but whatever they agreed to, I never earned another dime for it.

Then, something else that was never supposed to happen happened.

Chapter 13

"*NSYNC or swim"

I'm at my desk when I get a call from the account director on Chili's. "Great news!" she says. "Chili's just cut a deal with *NSYNC to sing the Baby Back Ribs song in a TV spot."

I am speechless, and not because it's "great news." My first thought is "Can this mistake of a song get any worse?" Working with a boy band — the artistic equivalence of advertising jingles — to promote Chili's baby back ribs made no sense at all. Did I miss the memo with new research revealing that the new target market for Chili's was preteen girls?

What the hell was Chili's thinking? And now, we had to come up with a script for it? And, actually go on a shoot with them? And, spend precious moments of the only life I have in a recording studio with them?

Advertising can be a cruel mistress. And, this mistress had become a bitch.

Despite my protestations, Chili's was pretty proud of themselves for signing *NSYNC. Once again, we were in a position where if we intended to keep the account, we had to figure out a way to turn this roadkill into a rose.

Starting with the script.

Fortunately, that quickly became a non-issue when a senior writer on the account came up with the idea of having individual members of the band stranded on a desert island, each one in turn singing the line "I want my baby back," as if they were pining for a lost love. After the fourth member sings the line, we would then cut to a shot of the entire group singing in unison to reveal what they were actually pining for: "ribs!"

The script evolved a bit after that to give it a semi-humorous ending, but just the fact that I have to describe it as semi-humorous is reason enough not to describe it any further. Semi-humorous is always a bad thing. Something is either funny or it's not.

To make matters worse, Chili's decided to recruit the band for an additional round of 15-second spots promoting their new "Chili's To-Go" service, rationalizing that we could shoot both spots at the same time. Given the need to shoot one spot on a desert island, that meant the To-Go spots would require a less extravagant location in order to stay in budget. As a result, the :15s were shot in a recording studio in Orlando, Florida.

Scripts approved, the next step was meeting with the band and getting the production wheels turning. After a preliminary meeting with the boys and their managers, it became apparent that we'd be dealing with some egos. Justin Timberlake was clearly the alpha male of the group, and the other members all knew it. The least appealing member of the group (name withheld because he knows who he is) was the biggest prima donna of them all. If he saw a script where Justin was slated to get more lines or on-camera time than the others, we heard about it from him first.

The first audio session with the boys took place in Las Vegas where the band recorded their rendition of the Baby Back Ribs song for the track that would accompany the TV spot. Because even boy musicians apparently sleep late, we didn't begin the session until 5 p.m., and other than the late start, it went well. By the time we wrapped things up around 3:00 a.m., it was clear why Justin was the star. While the other four did little more than phone in their performance and left the moment their parts were recorded, Justin hung around until the very end, looking for ways to plus the track — which he did with some beat-boxing improvised in the moment.

I got back to the hotel around 4 a.m. Slept for two hours. Then got up to catch a 7:30 flight back to Austin.

A week later we were in Orlando filming the To-Go :15s in studio before heading off to the Bahamas to shoot the desert island spot.

All-in-all it wasn't a terrible experience. Although there was one moment when one of *NSYNC's managers came up to the account director when we were filming the 15-second To-Go spots and told her that it was unacceptable for only three of the five boys to have a line while the other two sat silent. Given the fact that the spots were only 15 seconds long and three seconds of that was the logo, that left 12 seconds for dialogue. If all five members of the group were to speak, that would have meant giving each of them something to say that didn't go longer than 2.5 seconds each. Which clearly was not workable.

Dutifully, the account person brought the manager to me to deal with the issue. Right there. In the middle of the shoot. It was such a ridiculous request, I just looked at both of them and said, "Well, that's stupid, and we're not going to do it," thinking to myself "If you guys want to walk away from the gazillion dollars Chili's is paying you because we won't accommodate a request like that, walk."

Both the account director and the boy's manager looked stunned at my "unfiltered" response. Somewhat shell-shocked, they stood there staring at me with mouths agape for a few seconds before the manger responded, "Okay." Then, we all got back to work.

As for the Bahamas portion of the shoot, the only hiccup we experienced occurred as the result of Britney Spears's grandmother's passing. Justin and Britney were a couple back then, and he felt compelled to fly back to Louisiana for the funeral, which we managed to accommodate without upsetting the schedule.

Long story short, the spots weren't great — unless you were a huge *NSYNC fan, and then they were spectacular. I wish we could have made them better. But, looking back, by this time I was done with this whole chapter in my life.

It was time to close the book. But not before one more cosmic occurrence.

Chapter 14

"Are we rich yet?"

In its look back at advertising in the 20th century, *Advertising Age* named the "Chili's Baby Back Ribs Song" the number one earworm of the 90s. (To save you the trouble of looking it up, an "earworm" is a song that gets stuck in your head. It's usually not a good thing.)

At that point, the song just sort of took on a third life of its own. Since Fat Bastard debuted it in the second *Austin Powers* movie, it's appeared on *Saturday Night Live* (at least twice), *Will and Grace*, *South Park*, *My Wife and Kids*, *The Daily Show with Jon Stewart*, and *Scrubs*. Eddie Murphy sang it in his movie *The Money Tree*. Steve Carell sang it in *The Office*. Jamie Foxx belted it out on *The Jamie Foxx Show*. Scarlett Johansson did her version of it in a sketch about jingle writing on *Saturday Night Live*.

When Willie McCoy — the baritone who (from what I've read on the internet) sang "barbecue sauce" on the track — passed away, he had a barbecue-themed funeral where his body was placed in a large smoker while the song accompanied the procession to the stage. (Really. Google it.)

And, then came the advent of social media. The song has been covered in personal videos online more times than anyone can count. It's refusal to die has led Chili's to bring it back more times than you can shake a rib at.

When Chili's re-introduced the melody in 2017, I was living in the San Francisco Bay Area. For reasons I can only speculate, Chili's marketing director reached out to me to tell me they were donating $1,000 to the Berkeley Food Pantry in my name. Whatever the reason, it was very nice gesture that wasn't expected or necessary, but very much appreciated.

In its most recent reincarnation, Chili's hired Boyz II Men to perform the song in the Fall of 2023.

Chapter 15

"The song that refuses to die"

The song continues to resurrect even today in various places and ways — usually online. For the most part, people have nice things to say about it. Although, I do recall sitting in one focus group about the time the song took off and hearing one person say "If I hear that song one more time, I'm going to stick a fork in my eye."

So, how do I feel about it now? Still a bit perplexed that it captured the imagination of so many people the way it did. Glad a good number of people have nice memories of it. And, sorry that I couldn't find a way to make more money off it.

I've done a lot of work throughout my career of which I am quite proud. Given the way it has captured the imagination of so many people over the years, the Baby Back Ribs song lies somewhere in the middle. I certainly did a few things that I'm considerably less proud of. The thing is, I went for the fences with every project that landed on my desk. Even when it was a jingle.

I just never expected to clear the bases with one.

Then, there's the fact that I've never ordered, sampled, or eaten a plate of Chili's baby back ribs. But, that's a whole other story.

91

92

About The Cover

Cover design credit for *I Don't Want My Baby Back* goes to Larry Martin. An award-winning illustrator and designer, Larry was my first art director/partner at GSD&M. From one-off logos to full-on brand design projects, Larry has done it all. You can throw some work his way at larry@martincreativeinc.com. "But wait," you say, "I don't need any branding work. What I need is someone who can help me with the design/redesign of my new/current home." Well, Larry's got you there too. Just reach out to larry@martinhousedesigns.com. Same Larry. Different email address.

Made in the USA
Las Vegas, NV
04 May 2024

89485761R00059